A tale of three mothers

Marlon Deleon

BookLeaf Publishing

India | USA | UK

A tale of three mothers © 2024 Marlon Deleon

All rights reserved.

No part of this publication may be reproduced, stored in a retrieval system, or transmitted, in any form or by any means, electronic, mechanical, photocopying, recording or otherwise, without the prior written permission of the presenters.

Marlon Deleon asserts the moral right to be identified as author of this work.

Presentation by *BookLeaf Publishing*

Web: www.bookleafpub.com

E-mail: info@bookleafpub.com

ISBN: 9789358318814

First edition 2024

Dedicated to Cheekstah, Steve "The Jet", Farm Boy, and Fruhn.

ACKNOWLEDGEMENT

Thank you to Andrea who encouraged me to write again. Thank you to God for making dogs along with all that is good.

Zeke, The Bringer of Poems

War.
Peace.
Winged Messenger.
Jollity.
Old Age.
Magician.
Mystic.

The Planets are now aligned and this journey
can begin.
A brand new road is laid before me, time and
time again.

Defenestration of procrastination is finally
happening here.
A demonstration of new creations is starting to
appear.

An exploration of poetic styles is the thematic
route,
A smorgasbord of topics is what they are about.

If you know the list of words I started with
above,

You know that Holst does not include this planet
that we love.

And that is an important fact to note as you read
this book,
That everything among these words is worth a
second look.

Will they be about the love I hold for my new
dog?
Or will they hold a key to the next, like a
prologue.

You'll just have to read and see how these works
evolve.
I will have to figure out what stories to involve.

Thank you in advance for walking alongside me.
I hope to see you at the end of all this poetry.

Submarine Veteran

Sneaking around the oceans,
Under the noses of friends and foes alike.
Boys became men, or at least they thought they
did
Manning the stations they worked underway.
Air aplenty if everything ran well,
Running drills constantly to prepare for the
worst.
Inside this cold metal tube friendships were
formed,
Nicknames were bestowed and jokes were had
Everywhere we ported, debauchery got real bad.

Victory comes in many forms
Even in simply coming home.
The others may feel different from you,
Everyone has a unique experience.
Resources abound, if you know where to look.
All around the world, we have served.
Not everyone wants to be thanked.

The Two Brothers

There once were two boys, they were brothers,
Mom spurred them to fight one another.
She often compared and the older one fared
Much better than the one younger

Emotionally stunted, the young mother fronted
And pretended she didn't need help
Take it out on her boys, they made lots of noise
And then they'd lie limp like wet kelp.

Their teachers finally caught on
All year they wore sleeves that were long
They called CPS and they paid them a visit
To check on the house and who's in it.

The mother she put on a show,
And the tears, they started to flow.
The kids they were scared, not really prepared
For a performance that garnered kudos.

So she switched, physical to emotional
The prayers didn't help, nor devotionals.
She continued to hurt, her words became curt,
And she often left home without them.

Mom: A Haiku

5

Some say "Mom" means love
Those people have good mothers
I am an other

Parental Free Verse

Many preach about "the tragedy of broken
homes" and "single parent families"
How a child without a father is weaker than
most.
How single moms are more vulnerable than
married ones.
But let's not take this view to idolize "traditional
marriage" or the nuclear family.

I grew up with both bio parents in the home,
So I don't know that life.
But what I do know is different but similar.
Both parents existed and functioned,
But neither were there when it mattered.

One was quick to discipline and criticize,
But never to reassure or teach
The other knew how to work outside the home,
And provide the way they knew best - money

One pushed the kids to be the best at everything,
That anything less was a failure,
Preaching "If you're not first, you're last!"
Long before Reese Bobby sold it on the silver
screen

The other enabled the former.
Fueling her materialistic desires,
Encouraging her to get what she wants,
Never backing down from a request.

Now that I'm married and have kids of our own,
It becomes even more confusing,
Trying to understand the way they acted the way
they did.
The way they didn't act the way they didn't.

Loving children comes naturally,
And anger is taught and instilled.

If love is the primary language of the parent.

If love is not present, love cannot be given.
If laughter was never felt, laughter cannot be
shared.
If pain is what was felt, then pain must be given.

If parents don't push you to do better, then
someone else will.
It's just a matter of how you push them.
How you teach them.
How you show them.
How you love them.

Looking back I now thank them for what I
learned.
How not to be a parent.

Not just a Tool song

Sobriety is in the eye of the beholder.
Opportunities abound even when practicing
avoidance.
Be ready to be strong wherever you go.
Everyone has their own path.
Recovery is a daily choice.

A Simple Love

There once was a Schnauzer with ticks.
And maybe they thought he was mixed.
But he came home with us, without a big fuss.
And our faces received lots of licks

Do It For the Kids

Safety of the family comes first.
Unwilling to let go because of the blessings he
brings.
Rescued from a shelter.
Roped in by his antics and snuggles.
Energy matched from the initial meeting.
Nose to the ground he started to decline.
Deteriorating quickly, the vet had never seen this
before.
Early one morning he became aggressive with
the kids.
Returning him to the shelter was tough, but the
right move.

It Looks Different

12

Grief differs for all
It sinks deep down in your soul
Grief can break you down

Ezekiel 11:1-20 MSG
Erasure

[1] Then the Spirit picked me up and took me to the gate. There were twenty-five men standing at the gate. I recognized the leaders.

[2-3] God said, "Son of man, these are the men who draw. They say, 'We can make anything happen here. We're the choice pieces of meat in the soup pot.' [4] "Oppose them, son of man. Preach against them."

[5-6] Then the Spirit of God came upon me and told me what to say: "This is what God says: 'That's a fine public speech, but I know what you are thinking. You've murdered a lot.

[7-12] "Therefore this is what God, the Master, says: I'm throwing you out! You fear war, but war is what you're going to get. I'm bringing war against you. I'm throwing you out of this city, and punishing you good. I'll carry out judgment on you. Then you'll realize that I am God. I will carry out judgment on you at the borders and you'll realize that I am God, Instead

of following my ways, you've sunk to the level of the laws of the nations around you.'"

[13] I fell down, face to the ground, and prayed loudly.

[14-15] The answer from God came back: "Son of man, mean people exile you. This land has been given to us to own.'

[16-20] "Well, tell them this, I scattered you through other lands. All the same, I've gone. I will gather you back and give you back the obscene idols. I'll give you a new heart. I'll put a new spirit in you. I'll cut out your stone heart and replace it with a red-blooded, firm-muscled heart.

https://bible.com/bible/97/ezk.11.1.MSG

Zeke's Gotcha Day

My family has been asking for months.
Our kids having been asking for years.
My wife has been asking since before the kids
were born.

Health and safety came first.
We had a huge stipulation to satisfy.
The dog had to be hypoallergenic.

Goldendoodle
Labradoodle
Bernedoodle

We were surrounded with options.
All of our friends and family had dogs.
"Everyone has a dog but us," our daughter said.

Three years later the serious research began.
We priced supplies.
Crates, food, beds.

We met our friend's dog Bowser.
A Schnauzer.
Hypoallergenic.

And then I found Mario.
A Schnauzer mix.
Hypoallergenic.

We visited him the next day at the shelter.
I sat on the floor of the room with my son.
Mario came straight to me and sat in my lap.

That was the day we found our first dog.

The D List

Crate
Stuffie
Bed
Pee pads
Poop bags
Couch pad
Blanket
Lupine dog collar
Retractable Tug leash
50# Dry food
Canned Wet food
Bone-shaped treats
Coin-shaped treats
Clicker for training
Chew toys
Spiral yard stake
Tie-out
Food tray
Food and water bowls
Brush
Fine-tooth comb
Eye drops
Itraconazole oral
Doxycycline

This is what is left behind after the dog goes
away.

Memories
Pictures
Tears
Fur

We never thought we'd be looking for our
second dog so fast.

Farm Boy

I had never heard of Millersburg before you.
Come to think of it, I had never driven out that
far.
The whole family came along in our van.
And we knew this was more than a visit.

This was hope.
This was a new beginning.
This was another chance.

Driving down the long gravel driveway we saw
the farm house.
She walked across the yard to meet us.
It was biting cold, so she took us into the barn to
meet the crew.

You came to Sissy first.
You left and then you came back again.
That's when we brought you outside for solo
time.

We all got in our van and we headed to our
home.
Your new home.

Later I realized you didn't get to say goodbye.
You got in a van and you ended up somewhere
completely new.
All we want to do is love you.

Thanksgiving

Every year we take a trip to the brother's house
south of us.
We were unable to make the trip this year
because of work,
And friendship,
And a baby to be born.
All good things.

We were invited to friends' houses.
Different types of gatherings.
All with children.
All with full families.
All good things.

We didn't make any solid commitments.
We left ourselves an out
Because we didn't know the way things would
go.
Because we didn't know what we didn't know.
All good things.

Wednesday night we finally talked.
We finally confessed we were deferring to the
other.
We eventually shared what was on our hearts.

We simply wanted to stay home.
All good things.

So Thursday morning I went shopping.
I put in my noise muffling earplugs.
I got the cart.
And I shopped with efficiency.
All good things.

We cooked together.
We got the kids involved.
It took less than 3 hours.
We ate our first family Thanksgiving in our new
house.
All good things.

Rage Room

Recommended by a new friend.
A safe outlet for anger in a controlled
environment.
Gifted to me by my wife for my birthday.
Excellent experience to say the least.

Required materials are fragile items.
Overstock glasses and plates.
Out of date VHS and electronics.
Most wonderful way to get things out before I
meet with my new therapist next week.

Frantic Family Day (with Football)

The long weekend was good thus far.
Many laughs and smiles, fun was the star.
But after church, things went awry.
And we did our best to launch and fly.

Uncle and auntie both came to visit.
The kids cheered and were here for it.
The dog, however, did not fare well
For knocking at the door caused hell.

We had to crate the dog for a time.
Because he really lost his mind.
We tried hard to calm him down.
My smile transformed into a frown.

Then there was a spill on the cushion.
Coffee was spilled and Sissy was pushin
The mug that was left with some coffee to spare
Her legs flail about with lots of flair.

There was also much cleaning to be done.
But we still wanted to share in family fun.
We tried our out best to balance it out,
While Niners-Seahawks was a rout.

Eventually things calmed a bit.
It was time for bedtime fits.
The kids in jammies are ready for bed.
And they finally laid down their heads.

Mama and I sat in our seats.
What a day, we both were beat.
And finally we caught back up.
And snuggled up with our new pup.

One Week with Jerry Lee

"Stolen" isn't the right word, but it feels like it.
"Escaped" would mean you left without them
knowing.
Very excited children and parents drove away
with you.
Exiting the farm you spent the first 5 months of
your life on.
Now I am just realizing why the first few days
for you were so tough.

Dog days are shifting and you're becoming more
comfortable.
Amicable and affable would be an
understatement.
You follow me wherever I go in the house.
Soon enough we'll let you sleep on the couch.

Over Everything

"Family" is tough
For me to grasp as all good
"Blood" does not mean "love"

One in the hand is worth two in the can

Pre-dog life was straightforward—with toilets.
Outside BMs were known to me but not a part of
my everyday.
On the ground in a pile is the last place I planned
to be searching.
Puppers is doing well going outside, but man,
poop comes in many forms.

Before becoming a #DogDad I had changed
diapers for a few years.
Always ready for the smell and ready to wipe
the baby's bum.
Gagged a couple times when they were sick, but
you gotta do what you gotta do (do).
Squishy in my hand with a thin biodegradable
bag separating me from the canine waste.

More than six but less than seven

I once was an addict, one of many.
Who drank and smoked through many a penny.
I spent years wasting time, and definitely hurting
others,
While I worked out my pain, much caused by
my mother.

But one night I met a lady who sang.
And with her voice her energy rang.
I was professional in meeting her, but wanted
much more
I was goofy and also in recovery, far from a
bore.

We hung out one night, and ended up at The
Bucket,
We shared our wounds and trash and collectively
said, "Fuck it."
We kept hanging out despite others' words,
For we knew and we felt what we shared, saw,
and heard.

We visited churches, bars, bookstores, and a
bowling alley.

Our partnership grew with high peaks and low
valleys.
We each went to therapy and together went to
church.
To be fed, make friends, and to heal the hurt.

The seven year itch, not just a film from the
'50s.
But a belief that your nuptial bliss departs
swiftly.
Okay, maybe not swiftly, but still pretty quickly,
When you realize how much time has been
ticking.

Two months shy of seven years married,
And I know for a fact that Jesus does carry.
Because as much as she leaned on me, and I her,
We could not have done all this work in a blur.

It takes time and love and hurt and growth
To know who really harbors you most.
She's so much more than the simple word
"wife"
She brought me back to Him, she helped save
my life.

An Ode to Advocacy

Before we met it was obviously for yourself.
On our first date it was about Jesus.
Upon moving in together it was about safety.
When we got engaged it was about partnership.
When the test read "pregnant" it was about
security.
After we wed it was about adventuring together.
When you gave birth to our second it was about
new beginnings.
When I went to the hospital it was about mental
health.

Every time we moved it was about progress and
safety.
At the doctor's office you always knew to push
more than they wanted you to.
That time I quit before I had another lined up, it
was about safety and trust.
Buying the house was about building the future.
In communicating with the shelter you knew
there was more to his coughing.
While talking to professionals, some in higher
positions than us, you push to do better.

Advocating for others is one of the things you do best,
And I'm blessed and grateful to have passed the earlier test.

www.ingramcontent.com/pod-product-compliance
Lightning Source LLC
LaVergne TN
LVHW010932200726

843509LV00013B/2191